St. Augustine Puppy

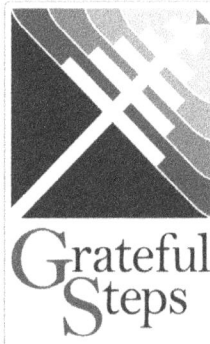

Grateful Steps Foundation
159 South Lexington Avenue
Asheville, North Carolina 28801

Krystal Collins

Library of Congress Control Number 2015904113
Collins, Krystal
St. Augustine Puppy
All photographs, unless otherwise specified,
are by Judy Collins
Casa Monica Hotel photograph courtesy of PhotoBucket

ISBN 1-978-935130-82-6 Paperback
Printed in the United States of America
Printer and Address

FIRST EDITION

www.gratefulsteps.org

To KC and Lilly
and to dog lovers everywhere

St. Augustine Puppy

Krystal Collins

Grateful Steps
Asheville, North Carolina

Once upon a time, there was a dog named Lilly. She was a sweet, little beagle with a bit of an attitude. She lived in Tennessee with her owner, Lynne, who loved her very much.

One day, Lynne came home with a surprise for Lilly. "Lilly, come here. I have something to show you," called Lynne.

Lilly jumped off the couch and onto Lynne's lap.

"What is it? What is it?" Lilly exclaimed.

Lynne hugged her tightly.

Lilly wiggled free and ran toward the door. "Did we get the gourmet treats I ordered?" She wagged her tail.

"No, bu . . ." Lynne paused. "You did what?"

Lilly slowly walked back into the room. "Nothing," she said quickly.

Lynne continued, "What I was going to say was that I got us two tickets to go to St. Augustine, Florida, so we can go along on a family vacation!"

Lynne was excited, but Lilly was not.

"Isn't that the place the Spanish guy discovered?" Lilly asked.

Lynne just rolled her eyes. "Yes, but call him by his name. He is Juan Ponce De Leon. He went to St. Augustine in the 1500s looking for the Fountain of Youth and—"

Lilly stopped her. "Lynne, if I jump into the Fountain of Youth, will I turn into a puppy again?"

Lynne just laughed. "Of course not. Now get some sleep. We're leaving tomorrow morning."

That night Lilly insisted on helping with the packing.

Early the next morning, they were off to St. Augustine.

Lilly did not enjoy the plane ride at all. "Hey! Let me out! I'm not a piece of luggage!" she cried. She complained the whole flight.

Finally she came out on the luggage carousel. Lynne quickly grabbed her and drove to the hotel.

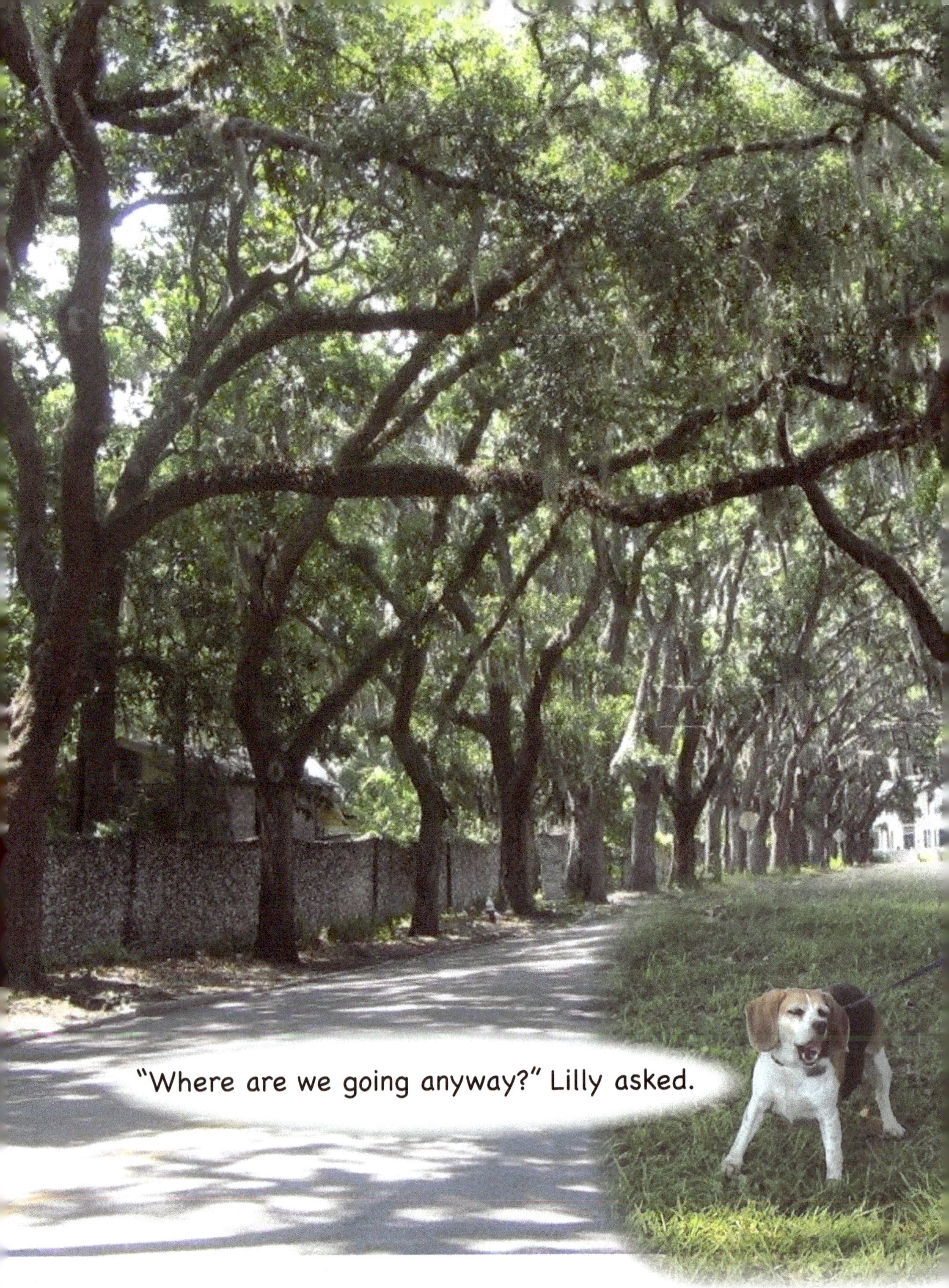

"Where are we going anyway?" Lilly asked.

"To the Casa Monica Hotel," Lynne explained, "It's the oldest hotel in St. Augustine."

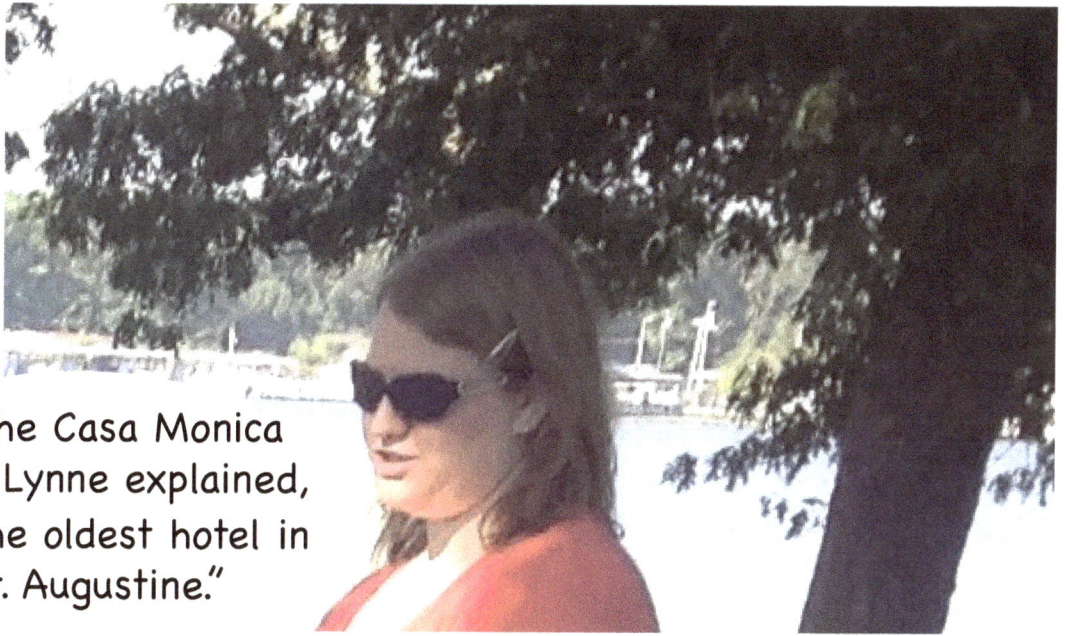

"Great," Lilly said. "My treats better arrive back at home while we're here."

Lynne just ignored her and checked into the hotel.

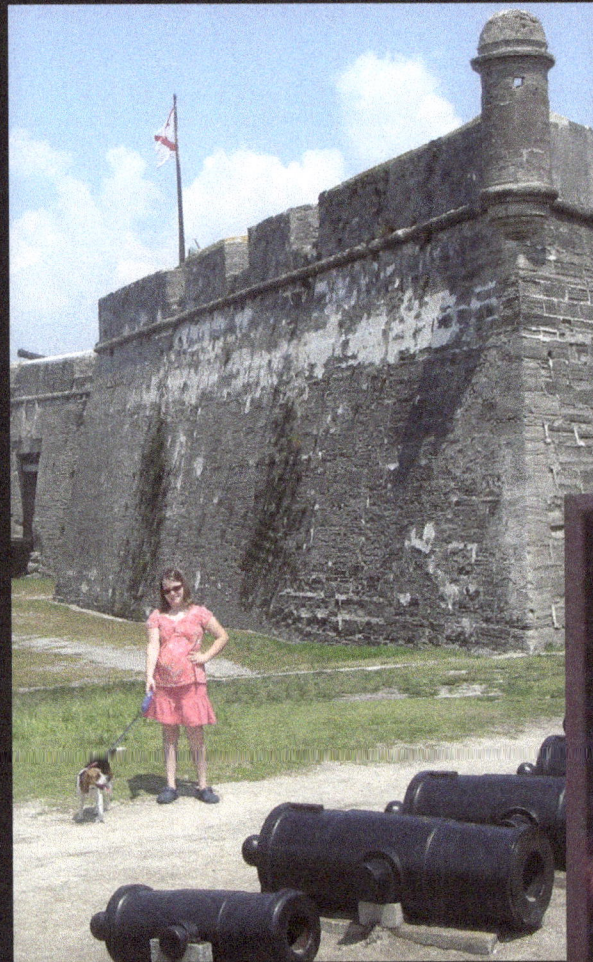

The next
week, Lynne
and Lilly
explored St.
Augustine.

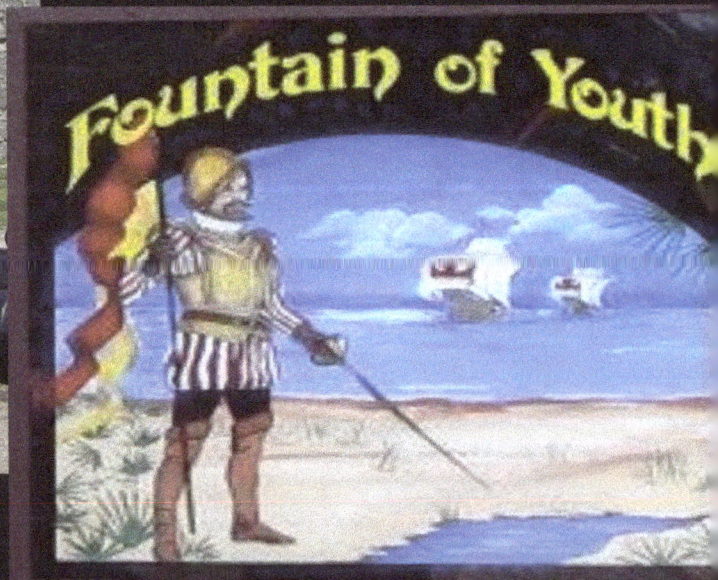

Fountain of Youth

Lilly jumped into the Fountain of Youth, but she only turned into a soaking wet dog.

She wasn't happy. "Let's just go back to the hotel," Lilly whined.

"It's okay," Lynne said. "We can go to the beach next if you want."

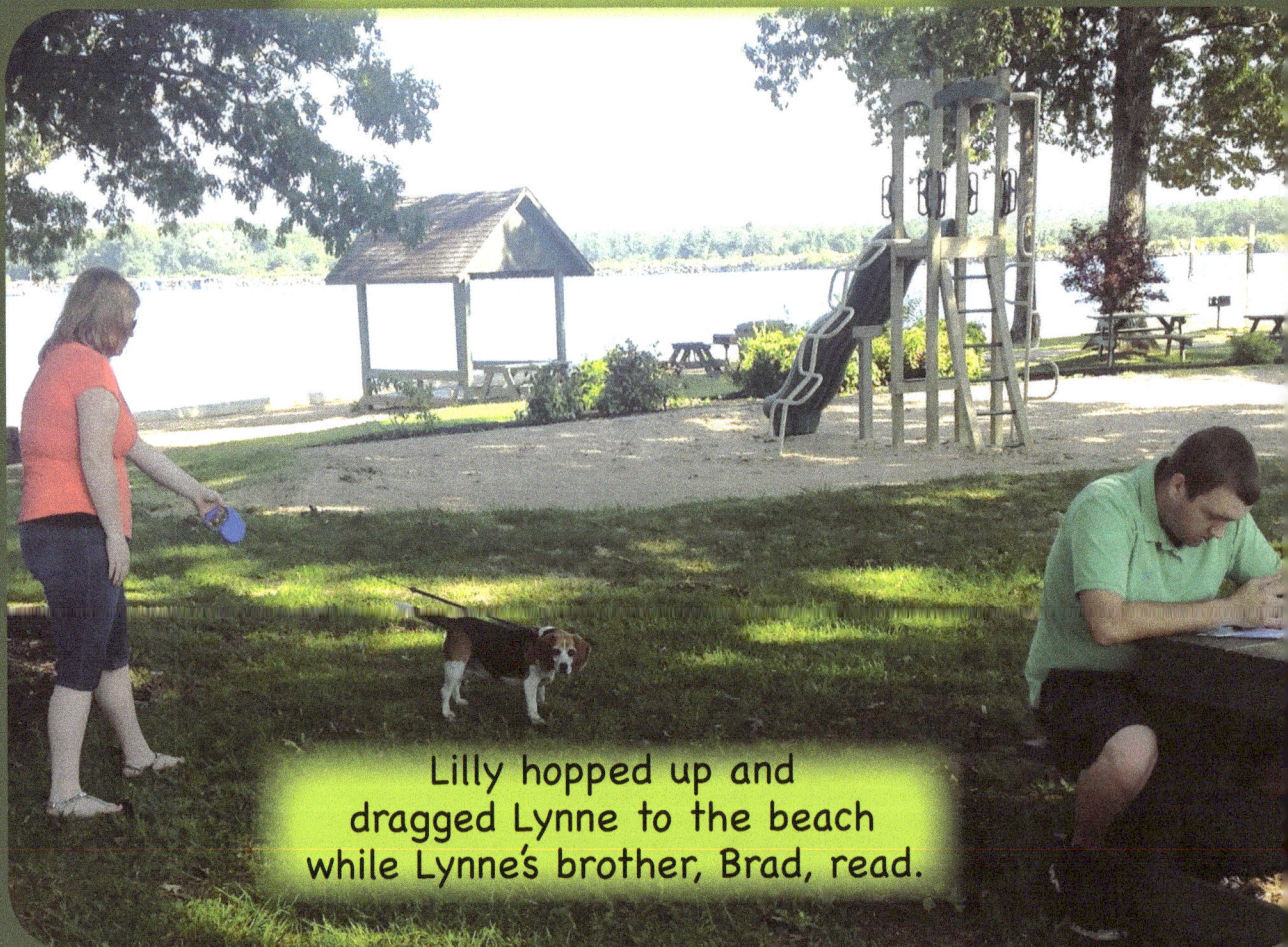

Lilly hopped up and dragged Lynne to the beach while Lynne's brother, Brad, read.

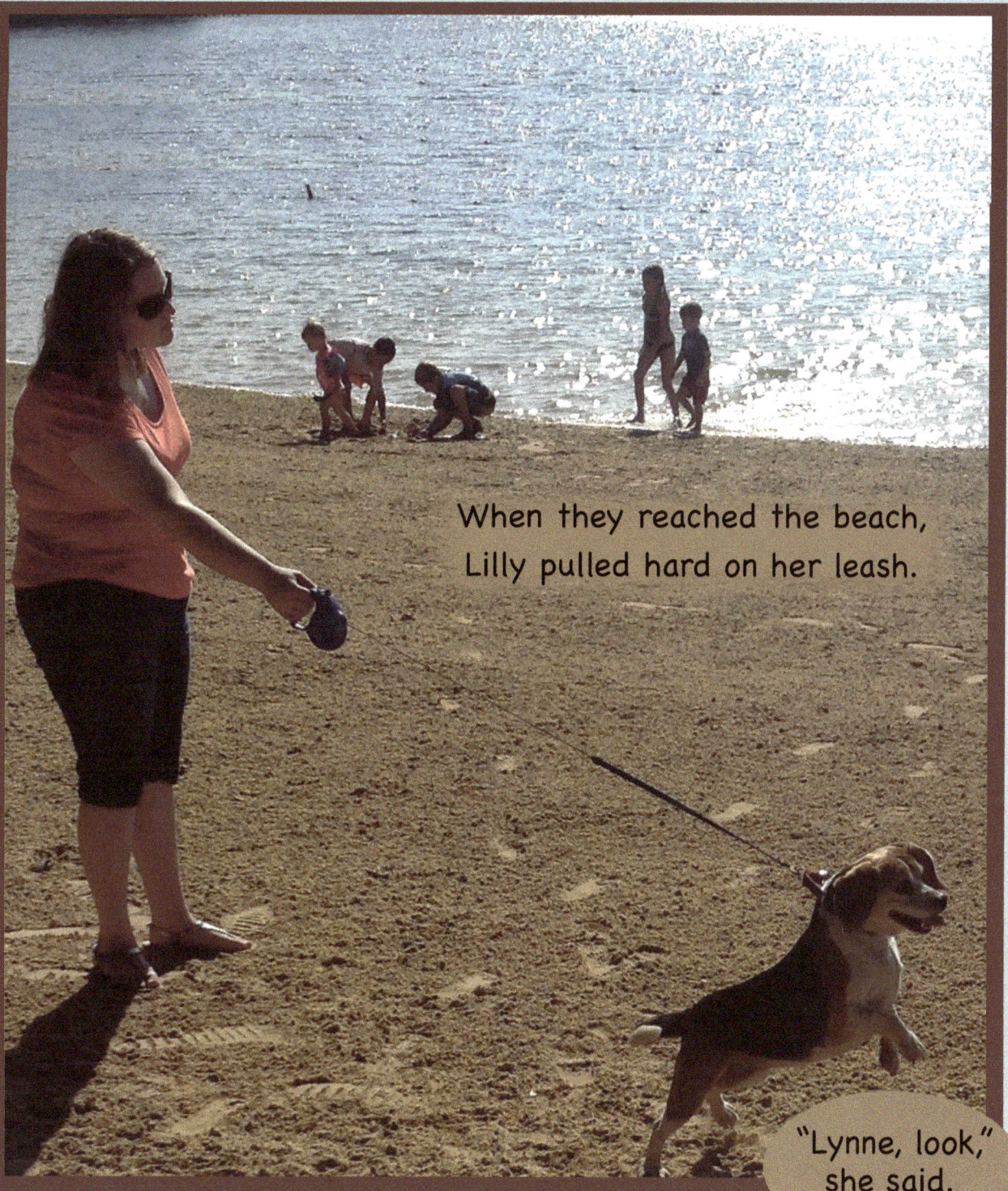

When they reached the beach,
Lilly pulled hard on her leash.

"Lynne, look,"
she said.

Lynne looked over to see a beagle at the beach. Lynne picked up Lilly and walked toward him.

"Hello. What's your name?" Lynne asked.

"My name is Leo," he replied.

Lynne smiled. "Nice to meet you, Leo. I'm Lynne and this is Lilly. Where's your owner?"

Leo looked down. He seemed sad.
"I don't have an owner.
I just live on the streets."

Lilly perked up. "How about you come live with us in Tennessee?" she asked.

"That's a great idea," Lynne said.

"How does that sound to you, Leo?"

Leo wagged his tail. "I would love to!" he exclaimed.

Lilly and Leo loved playing together at their Tennessee home.

A few months went by and they had six new puppies. They decided to name them Shadow, Buddy, Ellie May, KC, Brandy and Barney. Lilly hadn't been happy about going to St. Augustine, but now, looking at her little puppies, she wouldn't have missed it for a thousand treats.

Acknowledgments

Thanks to Mom, Dad and Grandma for all their love, support and encouragement throughout the whole process of this book.

Thanks to my brother, Brad Collins, for helping us with photographing the dogs at the beach.

Thanks to Hope and Abi Stone for letting me include Elvis in the book. He was Leo. I couldn't have done it without him!

Thanks to Daisy Filler, Dr. Leslie Eldridge, and all my wonderful teachers at CCHS for their support.

Thanks to all of you who were not mentioned but gave me support and encouragement during the work on this book. I appreciate you more than you will ever know.

Sponsor Page

Please visit our wonderful sponsors.
We appreciate their support.

About the Author

Krystal Collins lives with her family in Tennessee. She is a senior in high school. She plans to attend Tennessee Tech University and become a teacher after graduating college. She is President of BETA (National Honor Society) and President of Student Council. Krystal has acted in plays at her local playhouse and enjoys reading, photography, cooking, swimming and spending time with her family and dogs: Lilly (L) and KC (R). Krystal also volunteers at A Time 4 Paws, her local No-Kill adoption center for dogs and cats.

About the Puppy Star

Lilly is an 8-year-old beagle who joined Krystal's family when she was 3 months old. She actually took a trip to St. Augustine with Krystal and her family. That became the inspiration for Krystal to write this story. Lilly is a sweet beagle with an independent spirit. She loves to eat, sleep and play with her big brother, KC, a Chocolate Lab.

www.ingramcontent.com/pod-product-compliance
Lightning Source LLC
Chambersburg PA
CBHW041431040426
42445CB00020B/1982